Congratulations!
You're now a
fully fledged,

...You've worked hard, achieved the grades and the future looks bright...

...but what should you do next?

A note from the author

Do people tell you accountancy is boring? Don't you believe it! We've been dealing with an unbelievably diverse bunch of accountants at all levels for years, many of whom have become revered bastions of industry, banging down boardroom doors and slaying corporate dragons. But, we don't have to preach to the converted. You are probably newly or recently qualified and thinking about what career options you may have. It's good to be flexible and open to a range of options but, if we are really honest, it's always a lot better to have a plan. Of course, we don't mean you have to have a specific plan with details of your exact next role and where it will lead (and exactly when), but being aware of your options, the pros and cons of each, and the direction you would like to take from here, is really useful.

Put simply, the aim of this guide is to make sure that you don't make the mistake of getting caught up in the whirlwind of opportunities, suddenly finding yourself having had a series of interviews for weird and wonderful jobs that you really aren't sure were for you… and then having to consider a job offer that six months ago you wouldn't have dreamt of thinking about (this happens to more people than you would imagine – and very often results in a poorly thought out career move).

Remember, as flattering as the interest, offers of interviews and job offers might be, you've worked hard to get to this point in your career. Now is the time to take a moment to reflect and make a few well informed and well thought out decisions about what your future might look like.

We hope that you find this guide useful, objective and impartial. It's been written and structured to be simple to understand in nice, bite-sized chunks that can be read on the train, in a lunch hour or whenever you want really. So, without further ado, read on and start planning your career adventure.

Good luck.

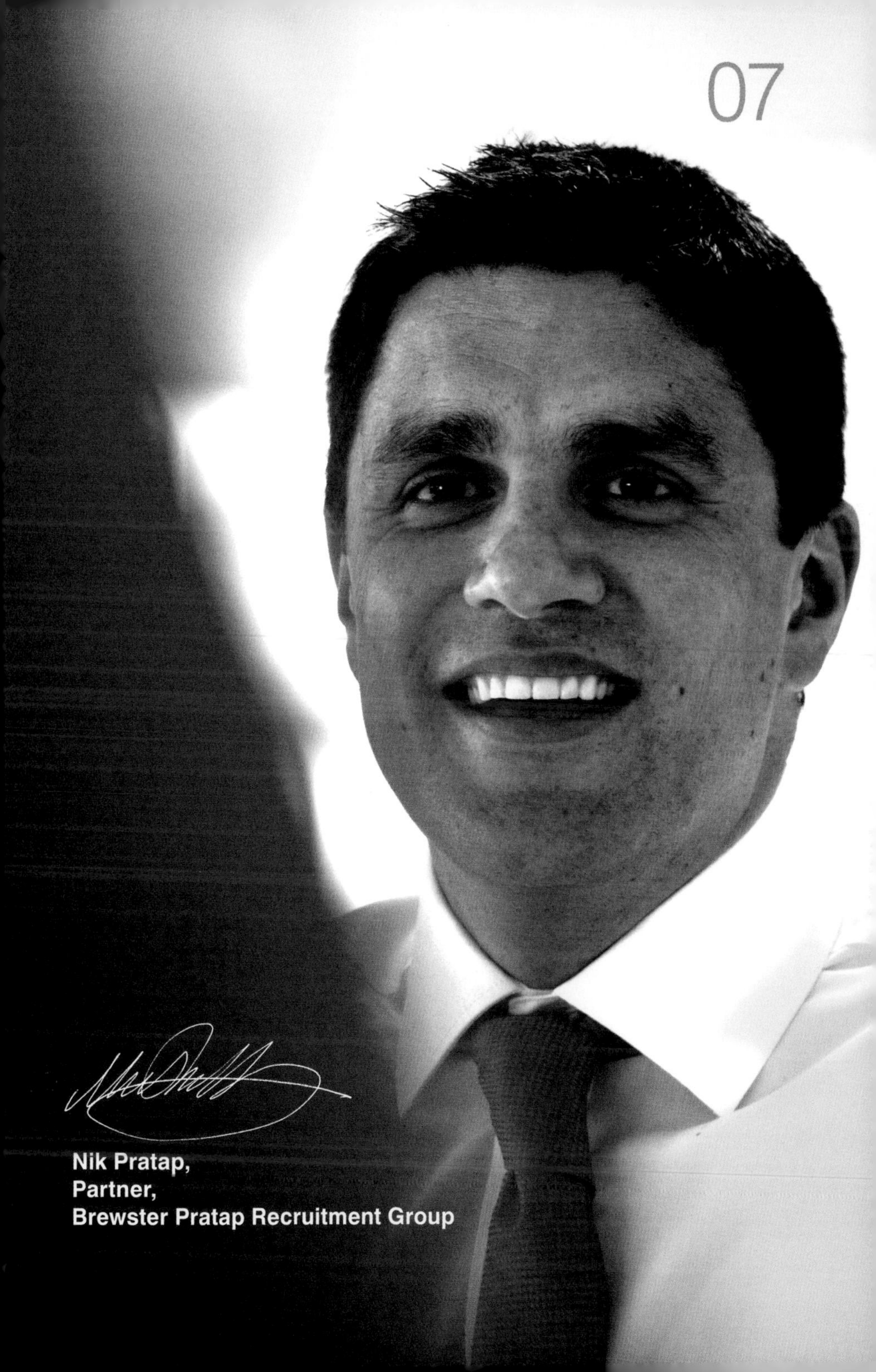

Nik Pratap,
Partner,
Brewster Pratap Recruitment Group

This guide is divided into two sections

(1) **Section 1** will give you a clearer picture of the options now available to you, including the most common roles with brief explanations.

2

Section 2 will give you some pointers on interview technique should you decide that you are going to enter the market.

Remember:

★ ★ ★

WE ARE HERE TO HELP

Our commitment to you is that if you have any questions, or would like some further clarification of any points covered in this guide – just get in touch. We won't try to encourage you to take a certain path   you will just get good, honest advice and support.

Section one

Career options

Which sector?

Having spent the past few years balancing hard work with study to make sure you pass your exams, newly-qualified Accountants are then faced with more career choices than at any other stage of their career, the first being, which sector you want to work within:

Commerce and industry

Qualified options in practice
(if that's the sector you have qualified in)

Not-for-profit, public & third sectors

The choice you make here will go a long way to shape the rest of your career. That is not to say that you cannot move between these three sectors later, however, **the significant majority of Accountants will remain within the sector they first choose on qualifying.**

Commerce and industry

The term 'commerce & industry' represents a huge range of diverse businesses. Careers in 'commerce & industry' open up to all candidates on qualification, regardless of which sector they have trained in. The term covers a vast range of businesses and choices for an NQ, for example:

- Corporate or SME
- Manufacturing, Construction, Technology, Retail, Service Sector
- PLC, Ltd company, private-equity owned

Without doubt, there are a great number of businesses out there that value the commercial and technical skills gained through your professional studies. And this isn't just limited to future financial roles. Many businesses actively look to promote qualified Accountants into operational management positions. In fact, many Chief Operations Officers (COOs) and Chief Executive Officers (CEOs) are indeed qualified Accountants and will have faced the same decision as you are now. This future breadth of opportunity very often makes a move into commerce and industry a compelling proposition.

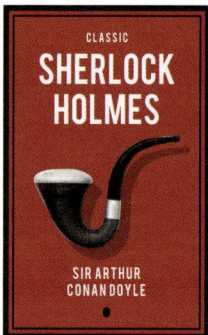

If this is your preferred route, but you haven't yet got your heart set on a particular sector or industry, you will need to take due diligence on the challenges that face a particular sector, both at a local and national level, as well as on a global scale (and you should do the same even if you have got some pre-determined ideas on your ideal sector). Thinking through the sort of challenges and opportunities a business will face in the next 3-5 years may help shape your thinking.

Another key point to remember is that the size of the business has a pretty obvious impact on the roles available (and indeed potential future options) but this is equally the case with different sectors. Our advice is that although job descriptions may look similar, you should ask some well positioned questions about what the scope of the role will be, and what the future prospects for further development are.

Don't forget

Very often the size of an organisation has a direct impact on the level of exposure the finance team have to the wider business.

Financial ?

Emotional ?

Logical ?

Qualified options
in public practice

Many Accountants who qualify in practice look to leave the sector in the
first year after qualifying. The challenge of balancing studies with the audit
season (and working away in many cases), is the reason that they have stayed
with the same employer for three years or more. The lure of so many other
opportunities provide the climate for this change to happen.

However, Accountants do not need to be in a hurry to leave the sector that has
shaped their career platform. Remember you are able to commit more time to
your job, now that the studies and exams are done. This means that there are
more opportunities for you to progress your career.

Some will stay in audit and accounting services, whilst picking up more
managerial duties, client responsibility and profile in the office. For others it
will be the lure of a move to a more specialist role such as:

- Audit
- Corporate Finance & Transaction Services
- Corporate Recovery
- Insolvency
- Taxation
- Forensics
- Management Consultancy

Those candidates who stay with their training provider, or who move to
another firm, gain the technical experience that will benefit their career,
working within an excellent network and preserving the opportunity to reach
the ultimate objective for any career in practice – a partnership opportunity.

Not-for-profit, public & third sectors

Newly qualified Accountants have chosen a career in the public and not-for-profit sectors to enjoy the satisfaction of reaching the objectives of their employer organisation, to enjoy the framework of personal development that exists in larger organisations and to enjoy a more 'project element' to their workload.

Historically, a good proportion of candidates who have opted to move into the public sector on qualifying chose to do so for the work-life balance and the attractive benefits package (final salary pensions, larger holiday allocations and flexi-time). Whilst some of these features do still exist and are valid attractions for any candidate, the expectations on finance departments have significantly increased in the last decade. 'Demanding & rewarding' is perhaps the best way of summarising these roles.

Choices are not as wide as in commerce and industry, but there are still many:

- Local and Central Government
- NHS
- Education
- Housing Associations
- Charities

The 'Age of Austerity' has had a negative impact on the attractiveness of the public sector as a career platform. Redundancies and a microscope on salaries and benefits are bound to have that effect! However, there is a lot more security in this sector than most may think. Costs have already been cut and now only 'essential' job roles exist in many organisations.

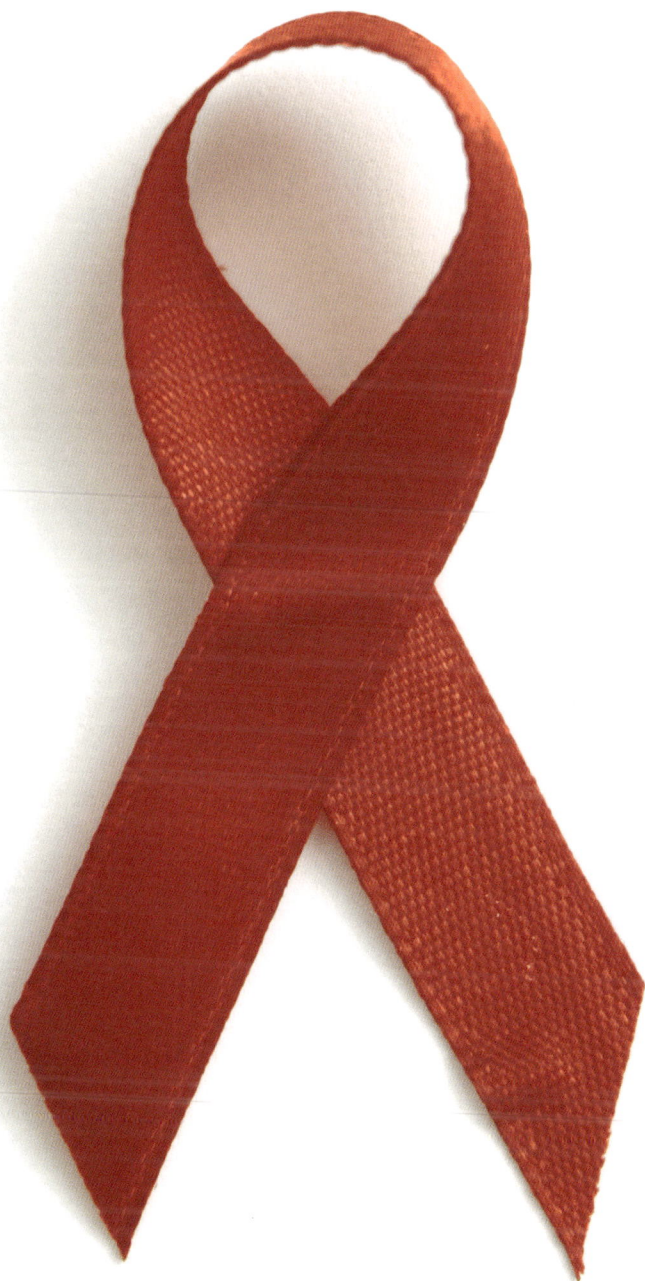

019

What suits you best?

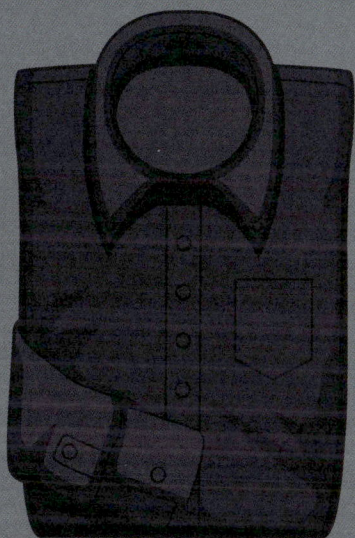

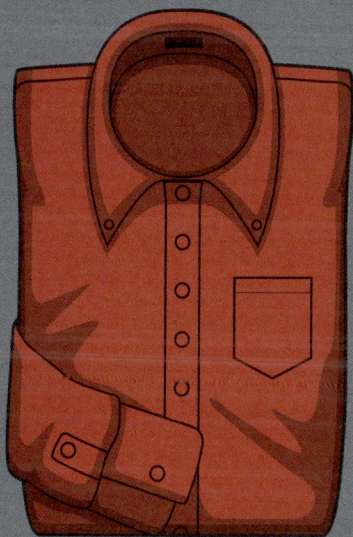
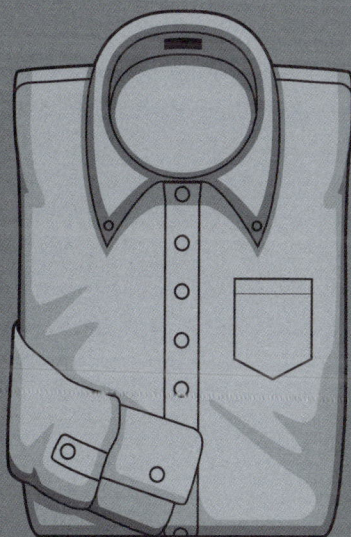

Management Accounting

Management accounting is used in order to inform an organisation to make key decisions and better manage and perform control functions. This very often involves the provision of financial and non-financial decision-making information to Managers. It involves partnering in management decision-making, planning, performance management systems and providing expertise in financial reporting control to assist management in the formulation and implementation of strategy. Management accounting information differs from financial accounting information in several ways.

These can be described as:

- Whilst shareholders, creditors, public regulators and other external bodies use financial accounting information, only Managers within the organisation use the typically confidential management accounting information.

- Whilst financial accounting information is historical by nature, management accounting information is primarily forward looking.

- Whilst financial accounting information is produced in accordance with general financial accounting standards, management account information is produced in accordance with the needs of management.

Management accounting activities will often impact both the finance team and wider business. The following list attempts to describe some typical tasks performed by Management Accountants:

- Price modelling
- Profitability
- Cost analysis
- Capital budgeting
- Strategic planning
- Sales forecasting
- Financial forecasting
- Annual budgeting
- Cost allocation
- Sales analysis
- Cost benefit analysis.

Financial, Business and Commercial Analysis

Financial, business and commercial analysis usually refers to an assessment of the viability, stability and profitability of a company, division, project, product or business process.

It will make use of financial statements, management information and reports, often developing ratios and business models to provide information, identify opportunities and make recommendations for change. This information will be presented to Senior Managers and Directors and provide the key basis for making informed business decisions.

Financial, Business and Commercial Analysis will often compare:

- Financial ratios of solvency
- Profitability
- Liquidity and stability using past performance across historical time periods for the same period
- Future performance using historical figures and financial techniques including present and future values and comparative performance between similar organisations, departments or projects.

Some typical uses may include decisions around how or whether to:

- Continue or discontinue operations or parts of a business
- Make or buy decisions in the manufacture of its products
- Acquire or rent machinery equipment or premises in the production and supply of goods
- Make recommendations regarding investing or lending capital and other assessments that allow management to make informed decisions on various alternatives in the conduct of its business.

The role of an Analyst will be to focus on improving and transforming business processes, providing more efficient ways of working, better supported through technology typically involving you in critically evaluating information from various sources. Often you will be required to provide timely and insightful management information to enable accelerated and improved fact based decision making that supports delivery of the strategic and operational plan of a business. A Commercial Analyst is usually part of Commercial Finance where it is viewed as a true business partner to the Sales, Operational and Commercial teams, providing analysis of business performance to enable effective business partnering, identifying trends and patterns in the market and identifying areas of improvement.

All Analyst roles will require a strong skill set, often advanced Excel and modelling skills and will provide real opportunities to liaise with both internal and external customers including Banks, Investors, Pricing teams and Operations and be involved in strategic decision making. Relationship building, commercial insight and process improvements are key.

Financial Control

The ultimate destination for the careers of many Accountants is a Financial Directorship. The role of a Financial Controller represents the summit for many Accountants, but is a stepping stone towards a Finance Director role for many others.

Financial control is predominantly responsible for overseeing the day-to-day operations of the Finance Department. This will typically report to a Finance Director or Chief Financial Officer but it is very common in small organisations for the Financial Controller to be the number one finance officer.

In addition to preparing reports, financial control responsibilities may also include compliance audits, internal controls, participating in the budgeting process and analysing financial data. Often Financial Controllers are involved in evaluating and selecting technology for use within a Finance Department and other related parts of an organisation. Financial controls are a critical part of any financial system. They ensure that resources are being correctly and effectively used and activities are correctly and accurately reported.

Poor financial controls can lead to the risk of resource being under used and inefficient or subject to theft, fraud or abuse. It is the responsibility of the Board of Directors to ensure that good financial controls are in place and it is the responsibility of management to ensure that controls are operating effectively.

The Financial Controller is often responsible for budgetary controls, including both revenue budgets and capital budgets, banking and cash controls, highlighting issues relating to cash balances, errors, loss and other misstatements, expenditure on purchasing controls, investment appraisal, payroll and personal controls as well as controls over assets.

Technical & Financial Accounting

Financial accounting is the field of accounting concerned with the analysis and reporting of financial transactions. Financial accountancy is governed by both local and international accounting standards. GAAP, is the standard framework for guidelines used within financial accounting in any given jurisdiction. It includes the standards, conventions and rules that Accountants follow in recording and summarising and in the preparation of financial statements.

IFRS, the International Financial Reporting Standards, is a set of international accounting standards stating how particular types of transactions and other events should be reported in financial statements. With IFRS becoming more widespread, consistency in financial reporting has increased between global organisations.

The objective of financial reporting is to provide financial information about the reporting entity that is useful to existing and potential investors and lenders as well as other creditors in making decisions about providing resources to the entity. Financial accounting generally refers to the preparation of financial statements that can be consumed by the public and relevant stakeholders. Financial accounting typically serves to produce general-purpose financial statements, produce information used by the management of the business and safer decision-making planning and performance evaluation. It also produces financial statements to meet regulatory requirements.

Whilst financial accounting is used to prepare accounting information for people, predominantly outside of the organisation, management accounting provides accounting information to help Managers make decisions to manage the business.

Internal Audit / Operational Review

Internal audit is the independent objective activity designed to add value and improve an organisation's operations. It brings a systematic, disciplined approach to evaluate and improve the effectiveness of risk management, control and governance processes. Internal audit is also the tool used to highlight deficiencies in, and improvements to, an organisation's governance, risk management and management controls by providing insight and recommendations based on analysis and assessment of data and business processes.

With a strong commitment to integrity and accountability, internal auditing provides senior management with an objective source of independent advice. The scope of internal auditing can be broad and may involve a diverse range of topics including, but by no means limited to, governance, risk assessment, risk management and management controls efficiency, effectiveness of operations, safeguarding of assets, the general reliability of financial management reporting as well as compliance with laws, regulations and other activities. Internal Auditors may also be involved in conducting both proactive and reactive fraud audits and fraud avoidance activities.

A key distinction between internal audit and other forms of accounting career, is that Internal Auditors are not responsible for the execution of company activities. They instead advise management and Directors how to better execute their responsibilities.

Internal audit activities are primarily directed at evaluating internal controls and are broadly defined as a process instructed by the entity's Board of Directors, management or others to provide assurance regarding the achievement of the following objectives:

- Effectiveness and efficiency of operations
- Reliability of financial management reporting
- Compliance with laws and regulations
- Safeguarding of assets.

Treasury

OK, let's imagine the scene, the economy has been typically turbulent, interest rates are low and you've been tasked with expanding an organisation's treasury coverage. This is your chance to really stretch those problem solving muscles, to not only manage the risk, but be carried out of the office shoulder high for negotiating a potentially huge saving or investment for the company, making the shareholders particularly pleased with you in the process.

Treasury management or treasury operations refer to the management of an organisation's holdings with the ultimate goal of managing a firm's liquidity and mitigating its operational and financial risk. The terms 'treasury management' and 'cash management' are sometimes used interchangeably, whilst, in fact, treasury management is larger and includes funding considerations and investment activities.

Treasury management is responsible for the administration and management of cash flow and includes an organisation's collections, disbursements, concentration, investment and funding activities as well as the creation and governance of policies and procedures used to manage risk successfully.

Taxation

Taxation, the bane of our lives or the very backbone of society? Income tax, capital gains tax, inheritance tax, wealth tax, corporate tax, whatever tax, they all help make society what it is today and help to give us street lights, health care, law enforcement, jails, fire departments, bin collections and even (boo hiss) traffic wardens. Think of a society without taxes and well, civilisation would degenerate into chaos. Yep, maybe even no more TV, an horrific thought. That's why taxation is a vital and important area to consider.

Committing to a career as a specialist in taxation will not appeal to every newly qualified Accountant but should be a real consideration for those who excelled in their tax modules and enjoy the nature of the work.

Opportunities in tax exist within all size of firms and within industry. Wherever you are working, the benefits of this career choice include; ongoing professional development (through the professional taxation exams), a clear career path to a Tax Manager or Partner route within practice, or in-house tax routes within the private sector. To be a champion of a technical area can provide real benefit to most businesses.

External Audit

Hundreds of Accountants will qualify in Yorkshire each year, with all of their practical experience gained in audit. A significant number will immediately plan their exit from the audit discipline for a move into one of the other specialist areas covered in this chapter. For many this is the right decision, but for many more, they are well advised to explore developing their careers in audit further (either within the same firm, or by moving to a different firm). The interviews with Andy Irvine and Andy Ward on pages 56 and 58 show some of the benefits of specialising further in the audit profession.

After January 1st 2016, any UK company with a turnover in excess of £10.2m per year, or with assets over £5.1m, is required to have their annual financial statements independently audited.

The audit process varies hugely based on the company involved – its size, sector, ownership, systems, marketplace and supply chain. Auditors have to be at the summit of understanding of statutory compliance, reporting standards and fundamental principles of accountancy. These are all skills that Accountants will learn as they study towards their qualification. Staying within audit after qualifying provides a long list of other benefits for all candidates to consider:

- More job satisfaction in providing value-added advice to clients
- The opportunity to manage audit teams and processes
- A clear career progression route up to Manager level and beyond – possibly up to Partner
- Specialise in a career that is internationally mobile and provides lots of opportunities to travel or relocate nationally or internationally
- The opportunity to network and actively be involved in business development

NOTHING TO
SEE HERE

Corporate Finance / Mergers & Acquisitions

The glamorous image of corporate finance attracts many trainee and newly qualified Accountants. Sharp suits, corporate hospitality and celebrating successful deals paint an enticing stereotype. Consequently, there is always a great deal of competition for corporate finance opportunities so you'll need to be determined and dedicated to develop and succeed in this arena.

Corporate finance is the area of accounting relating to the source of funding and capital structure of businesses in the actions that its Managers and Directors take to increase the value of the firm to its shareholders, as well as the tools used to allocate financial resources. The primary goal of corporate finance is to maximise, or increase, shareholder value through the analysis, recommendation, brokering and organising of different types of capital to achieve company objectives.

Is there anything as swashbuckling as a merger and acquisition, dealing with the buying, selling, dividing and combining of different companies to enable maximum shareholder return. Kapow! The roles of those in mergers and acquisitions will include a diverse range of activities, however the key aspects are those of business valuation financing options.

Corporate Recovery

OK, so on the face of it corporate recovery might sound like the type of arena that involves a lot of distressed business owners, staff potentially jumping ship and suppliers with blood boiling, demanding payment as a cloud hangs over the business in question. Well, that might be the premise for the start of a corporate recovery project, however, don't let that view sour your opinion. People working in corporate recovery can make a huge difference and help companies get back on their feet and start a new chapter.

Corporate recovery is a rescue undertaken by Accountants guiding businesses through troubled times. The business could have been under-performing for some time, or current economic conditions means that it is in a vulnerable cash state, with debts valued at more than its assets. Whatever the reason, corporate restructuring, or declaring the company insolvent, may be the only option remaining.

Usually qualified Accountants working with a portfolio of clients, your first aim would often be to help the company survive. This may be achieved through restructuring, which can involve streamlining operations, possibly salvaging some parts of the business and selling off other parts. You would look to turn things around and regenerate a more solid and successful business. In some cases, however, the only option might be to wind up the company, selling off assets to pay creditors. In this instance, you'd still be looking to secure the best possible outcome for stakeholders and employees, which can include recovering unpaid goods or money to pay lenders and suppliers.

Forensic Accounting

Forensic accounting is the use of accounting skills to investigate fraud or embezzlement and to analyse financial information for use in legal proceedings. Forensic Accountants are the detectives of the finance world and help investigate fraud and other financial misrepresentation.

The work of a Forensic Accountant is to enable lawyers, insurance companies and other clients to resolve disputes. Equally important is the ability to communicate financial information clearly and concisely in the courtroom.

Forensic Accountants are trained to look beyond the numbers and deal with the business realities of situations. Analysis, interpretation, summarisation and the presentation of complex financial and business related issues are prominent features of the profession. A Forensic Accountant will also be familiar with legal concepts and procedures.

Management Consultancy

Some of us are born to manage people, others are born to manage systems and yet more are born to manage strategy. Management Consultants are born to advise other Managers, to identify improvements and implement solutions.

Management consulting is the practice of helping organisations to improve their performance, operating primarily through the analysis of existing organisational problems and the development of plans for improvement.

As a qualified Accountant you will maintain the client facing aspect gained in audit, but have the chance to really influence profit generating areas. You will gain valuable business performance, strategic and systems related experiences, as well as seeing first-hand the intricacies of different industries. Whilst every consultancy project is uniquely challenging, you can be sure that you'll have the exposure and variety you need to rapidly develop your professional skills, network and career.

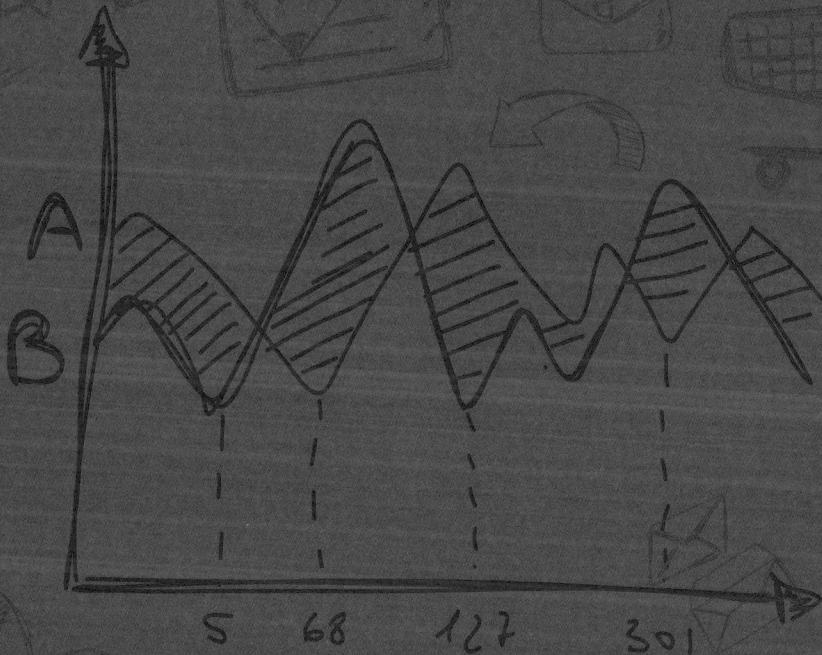

A

B

5   68   127   301

Been there...
got the t-shirt!

Case studies from those that have the experience, from newly qualified
Accountants to Finance Directors right up to a selection of Partners.

CASE STUDY

Newly qualified accountant

Tom Bell
BHP

Q What do you feel are the three most important attributes for a newly qualified Accountant looking to continue a career in public practice?

A I think that a willingness to learn and develop your technical skills is essential to any newly qualified Accountant looking to continue a career in public practice. Your whole career is built around understanding your clients' needs and sharing information, so good communication skills are also important. As well as this you need strong management and relationship skills, so that you can work with people and achieve shared goals.

Q What do you enjoy most about working in public practice?

A There's a lot I love about working in public practice. I really enjoy meeting and working with a wide variety of clients and industries. The variation in my role keeps it interesting. I also like business development and networking activities, through which I have been able to make a wide range of contacts who will be useful to keep in touch with as my career progresses.

Q **What has been the best moment of your career so far?**

A I was recently promoted to Assistant Manager in recognition of my work to date. This made me feel very proud and, if I had to choose just one, this is probably what I'd call the best moment of my career to date. I have also taken on the role of President of the local Chartered Accountant Student Society – which is another highlight.

Q **If you could give one piece of advice to a newly qualified Accountant, what would it be?**

A My advice for a newly qualified Accountant would be - always have an open mind about your role and the jobs you are working on and be prepared for anything!

Q **Has your working life changed since becoming a Manager?**

A Since becoming a Manager, I have learned to delegate better. I have also improved my soft skills to deal with a range of day-to-day issues. I find a lot of the reward comes from seeing those I am working with develop – something I hadn't really experienced before my promotion.

Q **If you could sum up your career in three words, what would they be?**

A Challenging, rewarding and flexible.

CASE STUDY

Financial Planning Manager

Karl Hearfield
Yorkshire Housing

Q What do you feel are the three most important attributes for a newly qualified looking to progress into a senior financial post?

A Adaptability – nothing is ever straight forward so you need to adapt what you have learnt or experienced to the situation. Nothing is ever the same twice.

Confidence – you need to show that you are applying your knowledge, and you need to do it with confidence. If you lack confidence people may not fully commit to your ideas or opinions as quickly, as they may think you don't fully understand the situation and subsequent consequences.

Interpersonal skills - the ability to work with all different types and levels of individuals throughout an organisation.

Q What do you enjoy most about your roles post qualification?

A Feeling I am able to have an impact on the strategy and direction of the companies I have worked in. Due to the positions I have held, I have had access to several executive teams, in and through the reports and models I have produced and I have directly influenced the direction of the business.

Q **What has been the best moment of your career so far?**

A Having a lead role in securing a £200m public bond issue, which at the time secured the second lowest rate in that sector.

Q **If you could give one piece of advice to a newly qualified Accountant, what would it be?**

A Believe in yourself. If you don't how are you going to persuade anybody else to.

Q **Has your working life changed since qualifying?**

A Not really, but I do have more control of my hours, so if I need to put a long day in to meet a deadline I can usually be more flexible over the next few days to try and get some of the time back.

Q **If you could sum up your career in three words, what would they be?**

A Challenging, rewarding and surprising – I never thought I would be where I am when I started out.

CASE STUDY

Finance Director

Janet Pryke
JNP Consultancy Ltd

Q **What do you feel are the three most important attributes for an Accountant to have, if they want to become a Finance Director?**

A Integrity – an absolute must and would always be the first on my list of requirements.

Commitment – you have to stand out in a crowd and show that you are committed to your employer and the role you are performing. This doesn't necessarily mean long hours but working hard and smart when at work.

Ability to multi-task / prioritise – often in finance there are several stakeholders requiring information, so the ability to service all parties and manage expectations are important attributes.

Q **What do you enjoy most about working within the commercial sector?**

A The variety of organisations that I have worked in have made for a very interesting career, it has never been boring.

Q **What has been the best moment of your career so far?**

A Starting my own business to provide interim support to organisations that have a short term need for my expertise. I have been working for myself since early 2013 and have worked within several different sectors and thoroughly enjoyed the experience.

Q **If you could give one piece of advice to a newly qualified Accountant, what would it be?**

A Always challenge yourself and learn as much about the business you are working in as you can, both inside and outside of the Finance Department. This will help with your business knowledge and give you a better understanding of the day-to-day issues other colleagues have to deal with. When working as a Finance Director there will be much more involvement with other departments, so the sooner you understand how the business operates, the sooner you can start thinking about how you can add value.

Q **How has your working life changed since becoming a Finance Director?**

A I now have staff to prepare the financial statements; it has become much more interesting and has meant that I can spend most of my time working with internal and external stakeholders to add value to the business.

Q **If you could sum up your career in three words, what would they be?**

A Rewarding, diverse and enjoyable.

CASE STUDY

Group Finance Director

Darren Marr
Leo Group Limited

Q What do you feel are the three most important attributes for an Accountant to have, if they want to become a Finance Director?

A Leadership skills

Honesty and integrity

The ability to communicate clearly

Q What do you enjoy most about working within the commercial sector?

A I am passionate about business generally, so this provides me with an opportunity to experience and understand the market, industry sector and the wider environment in which an organisation operates. This 'real world' aspect of the role touches upon the current economic and political issues, nationally and internationally, that affect businesses. There is a constant need to be innovative and strive for continuous improvement, to drive the business forward. Commercial finance is at the heart of industry and commerce, requiring interaction with all parts of the business and making a tangible difference to the performance of the company.

Q **What has been the best moment of your career so far?**

A As Group Financial Controller in a previous role, I led and successfully completed the 'one company project', where we simultaneously:

- Hived-up all of the 11 trading companies into a single entity, at the financial year end
- Implemented a new fully integrated ERP system throughout the group
- Relocated all of the site based ledger accounts staff and established a head office transactional shared service centre.

Q **If you could give one piece of advice to a newly qualified Accountant, what would it be?**

A Don't chase the money or the status of a role. Practical experience, exposure to new challenges and the right attitude and commitment are vital in ensuring that you develop both technically and personally. Following this, the exciting and rewarding roles will follow.

Q **How has your working life changed since becoming a Financial Director?**

A The 'buck stops with me' – this brings great responsibility

People see me as a leader and therefore look to me for inspiration, guidance and support

I have a direct impact upon the current performance and future direction of the business

9-5 doesn't exist and it is much harder to get the work/life balance

Q **If you could sum up your career in three words, what would they be?**

A Rewarding, varied and achievement

CASE STUDY

Partner

Andy Irvine
Shorts Chartered Accountants

Q What are the three most important attributes for an accountant to have if they want to become a Partner within an accountancy practice?

A For the individual and their business to be successful over the long term, you need to be able to step back from day-to-day matters to think and plan strategically for the future, both in terms of your own career, and ultimately, the firm you become a Partner of.

It's about being more than just technically proficient. Business is all about people and relationships. To become a trusted adviser to your clients and have a dedicated and motivated workforce you need to have strong interpersonal skills and be willing to listen, just as well as you give advice.

In my view, there is no point in becoming a Partner if you don't enjoy it when you get there. I believe that you need to be clear what your core values are and not compromise on those. In that way the right candidate will find the right role, within the right firm for them.

Q **What do you enjoy most about working within the profession?**

A The diverse nature of my various clients, helping them with their issues (which very often are not accounting related at all) and forging strong, long term relationships with clients and staff.

Q **What has been the best moment of your career so far?**

A Receiving the telephone call to confirm that I had been accepted for a two year secondment in Auckland, New Zealand with PwC.

Q **If you could give one piece of advice to a newly qualified Accountant, what would it be?**

A It's a great qualification, which opens up lots of opportunities. Don't rush into your next career move without thinking through the next two or three moves and ultimately where you might end up. Above all, think strategically.

Q **Has your working life changed since becoming a Partner?**

A Becoming a Partner at Shorts has been great for me. I make sure I get my work/life balance right, no overtime (one of my core values) and, as well as looking after some great clients, I get to contribute to running a rapidly growing, successful, progressive firm.

Q **If you could sum up your career in three words, what would they be?**

A Rewarding, diverse and fun.

CASE STUDY

Partner

Andy Ward
PwC

Q **What are the three most important attributes for an Accountant to have if they want to become a Partner within an accountancy practice?**

A I would say they need to be able to build relationships, embrace being a leader, and overall have the intuition to 'do the right thing'.

Q **What do you enjoy most about working within the profession?**

A The variety of what I do – everything from business development, problem solving, to nurturing and developing your team. I have to make decisions that make sure the business is in great shape for the next generation.

Q **What has been the best moment of your career so far?**

A So many fun and great moments (as well as the inevitable difficult times) but it would have to be being part of US IPO transaction when I lived in Houston, Texas.

Q **If you could give one piece of advice to a newly qualified Accountant, what would it be?**

A Have an appetite for development and make sure you enjoy yourself on the way.

Q **Has your working life changed since becoming a Partner?**

A Yes, my working day/evening can be really varied and can either be back to back meetings, or time to reflect and develop strategy. Some really contrasting days.

Q **If you could sum up your career in three words, what would they be?**

A Rollercoaster, surprising and fulfilling.

Section two

Entering the market

Firstly, you'll need to create a successful CV

As technology makes it even easier to apply for a job, the number of CVs for each vacancy has risen. The following pages illustrate how to structure your CV to stand out.

A CV is a vehicle to articulate past achievements, accomplishments and credentials, as well as conveying your personal brand to a potential new organisation. The CV is potentially the first touch-point that the organisation might have with an applicant, so it is imperative that it conveys you as a genuine contender, who is more than capable of adding value to the company.

Many candidates tend to submit a list of historical roles, activities and career details that they believe are crucial to the role. The problem is that most of the other 100 applicants will have done the same and the reader only has a short time, sometimes just a minute or two, to make an initial judgement about who they want to see.

Conveying your present skill set is vital. This is key to a successful CV, so streamline your career history into a format that is easily and quickly digestible by the reader and shows that you can deliver in your next role.

Brewster Pratap are experts in offering a compelling profile of our candidates and their potential. The following pages illustrate the career highlights of a typical newly qualified candidate CV as a general basis for your CV. Of course there will be occasions when the CV needs to be tailored in a more specific manner, however this guide is designed to enhance your chances of getting your 'foot in the door'.

We hope that this guide is useful. If you'd like any further assistance, please contact us.

Sample CV for candidates from industry or public sector
Pt 1

Sarah Howe
Newly Qualified Management Accountant

A relevant headline will immediately grab the attention of the reader.

Personal profile

- A **CIMA qualified Accountant** with experience of working in two growing companies in the retail and manufacturing sectors.
- Experienced in working with the **commercial and operational** sides of the business to provide monthly management information, variance analysis and assist in effective decision-making.
- Strong **communication and team-working skills**, both of which have been tested successfully in demanding situations.

Personal profile should be edited for each application, be succinct, and to the point.

"Sarah has been an excellent member of my Management Accounting Team for the past two years. Very comfortable communicator, strong Excel skills and a natural desire to get involved in the business have been the core ingredients to her success"

Finance Director, QWERT plc

Incorporating comments from referees or endorsements has a significant impact in a CV.

Key skills

- Management Accounting
- Budgets & Forecasts
- Annual Statutory Accounts (UK GAAP)
- VAT
- Payroll
- Stock Reporting

Listing key skills can help avoid repetition of skills in different job roles, reducing the length of the CV and maximising impact.

Sample CV **for candidates from industry or public sector**
Pt 2

Sarah Howe
Newly Qualified Management Accountant

Career details:

Employer One Ltd   **Jan 2014 to date**

Employer One is a private equity backed business, manufacturing building products for a national and international market. Turnover in 2006 was £23m with EBITDA of £250k. Turnover for 2013 was £35m with EBITDA of £3.4m.

Management Accountant

Achievements

- Successfully reduced the time-scale for producing monthly management accounts from 8 days to 3 days.
- Established a new meeting timetable with the junior Management Team to present the monthly management accounts to improve communication.
- Assisted the Finance Director in the successful implementation of SAP v1 within expected time-scales.
- …etc…

Employer Two plc   **Jan 2010 to Dec 2013**

Employer Two plc is an AIM listed retail business with a network of 65 sites across the UK and Ireland. During my seven years here, the turnover ranged from £67m to £98m with profits peaking at £5.6m. The business successfully listed in June 2000.

August 2002 to December 2005 – Assistant Accountant

Duties & achievements

- Successfully completed my CIMA training contract (first time passes).
- Reporting to the Management Accountant, I was part of a team of 4 producing the monthly management accounts.

Describe the business activity, the financial performance and change during your employment.

Link all experience to achievements rather than duties.

Split employment into each role to demonstrate progression within each stage of employment.

Sample CV **for candidates from industry or public sector**
Pt 3

Sarah Howe
Newly Qualified Management Accountant

Earlier Career Details

June 2009 to Aug 2009 – Temp Purchase Ledger Clerk, Employer 3 plc

2007 to 2008 – Part Time Waiter at Royal County Hotel

'Briefly' list your early career history.

Qualifications

CIMA qualified (First time passes) 2013

BA (Hons) Economics 2010, Sheffield Hallam University

3 A-Levels (BBB) and 10 GCSEs (All graded C or above) Stockton School

Include recent and more advanced qualifications that are pertinent to the role.

Personal Detail

Duke of Edinburgh Gold Award, 2009

Treasurer of Students Union, 2009

Keep fit regularly – regular gym user, cross country runner and past member of Sheffield Hallam University Athletics Team

Add interests to give your CV impact. This is an area to demonstrate your personality, however, only use interests that make you stand out.

Contact details

14, High Street, Newcastle, NE4 6HY

07986 123456

senior@hotmail.com

Make sure contact details are correct and up-to-date.

Never lie when writing your CV or attempt to suggest you're something that you're not. Lying is particularly bad form and will instantly tarnish your reputation.

HOT TIP

Everything on your CV is true...right?

RESUME

Sample CV **for candidates from practice**
Pt 1

Mark Ward
Newly Qualified ACA looking for first move into industry

A relevant headline will immediately grab the attention of the reader.

Personal profile

- **ACA qualified** with experience of training within one of the region's leading independent firms of Accountants.
- Audited a range of clients from SMEs to corporates, covering US and UK GAAP, across a range of sectors and ownership structures.
- **Strong communication and team-working skills**, both of which have been tested successfully in demanding situations.

Personal profile should be edited for each application, be succinct, and to the point.

"Mark has been an excellent member of my audit team for the past two years. Very comfortable communicator, strong Excel skills and a natural desire to get involved in the business have been the core ingredients to his success"

Audit Manager, Employer One

Incorporating comments from referees or endorsements has a significant impact in a CV.

Key skills

- Audit
- IFRS
- Annual Statutory Accounts (UK GAAP)
- Group Consolidations
- Management Accounts
- Stock Reporting

Listing key skills can help avoid repetition of skills in different job roles, reducing the length of the CV and maximising impact.

Sample CV **for candidates from practice**
Pt 2

Mark Ward
Newly Qualified ACA looking for first move into industry

A relevant headline will immediately grab the attention of the reader.

Career details:

Employer One   **Jan 2013 to date**

Employer One is a firm of Chartered Accountants based in Sheffield with 75 members of staff.

Describe the business activity, the financial performance and change during you employment.

Audit Senior

Achievements

- Producing financial statements in accordance with UK GAAP and IFRS.
- Taking a lead role on audit engagements, with a team of up to 4 people, providing technical advice, mentoring and motivation of staff.
- Producing key deliverables for clients, summarising their audit findings and any control recommendations identified.
- Co-ordinating the attendance of approximately 30 A Level students to the Sheffield office. Full management of the project encompassing building relationships with local schools, structuring and planning the activities for the day, ensuring sufficient staffing from the Sheffield team, and debriefing to consider feedback and points forward for the following year.
- …etc…

Link all experience to achievements rather than duties.

Employer Two plc   **Jan 2010 to Dec 2013**

Employer Two plc is an international Assurance, Tax and Advisory firm.

August 2002 to December 2005 – Semi Senior

Duties & achievements

- Successfully completed by ACA training contract (first time passes).
- Audit of UK companies in accordance with UK auditing standards. Clients vary in size from £50-£250m turnover.
- Assisting in the preparation of corporation tax computations for small and medium UK companies, while on secondment to the Taxation Department.

Split employment into each role to demonstrate progression within each stage of employment.

Sample CV **for candidates from practice**
Pt 3

Mark Ward
Newly Qualified ACA looking for first move into industry

Earlier Career Details

June 2009 to Aug 2009 – Temp Purchase Ledger Clerk, Employer 3 plc

2006 to 2008 – Part Time Waiter at Royal County Hotel

'Briefly' list your early career history.

Qualifications

ACA qualified (First time passes) 2015

BA (Hons) Economics 2009, Sheffield Hallam University

3 A-Levels (BBB) and 10 GCSEs (All graded C or above) Stockton School

Include recent and more advanced qualifications that are pertinent to the role.

Personal Detail

Duke of Edinburgh Gold Award, 2009

Treasurer of Students Union, 2008

Keep fit regularly – regular gym user, cross country runner and past member of Sheffield Hallam University Athletics team

Add interests to give your CV impact. This is an area to demonstrate your personality, however, only use interests that make you stand out.

Contact details

14, High Street, Newcastle, NE4 6HY

07986 123456

senior@hotmail.com

Make sure contact details are correct and up-to-date.

Interview
basics

Don't ever forget – an interview is a two-way exchange of information

Obviously the interviewer is trying to find out about you, but you're also sizing them up, forming an impression of what it will be like to work with and for them, and collecting information to aid your decision as to whether you would like to join them. Given this two-way exchange you must be clear about what the interviewer learns about you.

The interviewer's agenda is usually to:

- Get a clearer picture of your experiences and capabilities
- Hear examples of how you worked in the past, what you really did and how you really did it
- Get an accurate idea of how you match their needs (both in the short and longer term)
- Compare you with other good applicants.

So, with this in mind, your aim should always be to:

- Present compelling evidence of your experience, skills, knowledge and transferable skills and your ability to deliver (both in the short and medium term)
- Reveal your personality and style (your personal brand) and your ability to work well with others
- Assess how the organisation meets your needs on job content, working environment, culture, style and career prospects
- Get the interviewers / organisation excited about employing you.

An interviewer will be looking at your competence (have you got the knowledge, experience and skills to do the job?) and your compatibility (does your working style fit the organisation and particularly the people you will be working with?) together with your potential to develop.

Typically, other than an initial 'first impressions' assessment, at the first interview, the main focus will be evaluating your competence. This is usually pretty evident as their main agenda, although they may start to form an opinion on compatibility as well. In follow-up interviews your compatibility is likely to be a much more important aspect of the discussion.

As a newly qualified Accountant you may be familiar with the interview process, however it is useful to consider what the interviewer is seeking, drawing on any practical experience you may have had interviewing someone else in the past.

If you have been involved in the interview process previously, consider what impressed you about the people who were successful at interview. Conversely, what mistakes did the candidates make that failed to give a good impression, why they didn't do themselves justice or let themselves down.

The best interviews are performed by those who have done their homework on the vacancy, on the business and, as much as possible, the culture (more on this later). It is important to give a good impression that is consistent with the one that has been created on paper.

Research

It should go without saying, but you need to be well prepared and fully briefed on the organisation you are visiting.

As a minimum, always conduct these interview 'pre-flight checks'

Make sure you are familiar with the job description and understand the person specification. Draw up a list of questions, observations and points for discussion.

Make sure you confirm your attendance (either directly or with the recruitment company).

Check the location (obvious, but don't make the mistake of going to the wrong site of large corporates or use sat nav and realise that the postcode address takes you to the local sorting office). Yes, it happens frequently. Also make sure you're aware of car parking arrangements.

Make sure you know the anticipated length and type of job interview, what sort of interview it is (e.g. panel interview) and whether there will be any tests.

If a recruitment consultancy is involved, get all the background information you can before your interview about the client/company (why is the role available and why have they been instructed etc).

Make sure you know the names and job titles of the interviewers and, if possible, look them up on 'LinkedIn' to see what you can find out about them (don't worry about them knowing you've looked them up - it proves you've done your homework).

Make sure you have done some relevant background research, for example; statutory accounts, most recent share price, a thorough run through the business website, a 'Google' search of news articles about the business, a similar search on the business' industry sector.

At the interview

LISTEN to the question

Listen to questions carefully and respond as naturally as you can. Sounds really simple, doesn't it, however it's often the number one reason why people don't progress through an interview process.

In particular, take care not to answer the question that you wished the interviewer had asked you and never answer a question by spewing out a monologue of everything you want the interviewer to learn about you. Just listen carefully and answer the question. The preparation you have done will pay off here as you'll make a better impression if you can present relevant information without being prompted and without too much thinking time. But don't just rely on the interviewers' questions to guide you. Ask questions (and have some prepared).

Some questions you can ask:

- What would you like the person you appoint to achieve in the first year?
- What does success look like for this position?
- What is the biggest challenge facing the successful person?
- What is the biggest challenge facing the business?
- Have the objectives of the business changed recently and, if so, why?
- Have there been any major organisational changes recently?
- What would you say are the most exciting things about this business / opportunity?
- How do you see your market evolving over the next 3 years?

DON'T turn up empty handed

There are some things that are useful to have with you in the interview, however, keep them stored away in something professional that you can take into the meeting with you until they are needed. A conference folder is a way of storing any papers that you want to take to the interview and is always better than rummaging in a packed briefcase or handbag.

We believe you should always take:

- Any information about the job you may have

- The names and titles of the interviewers

- The company phone number and/or the mobile number of your Recruitment Consultant (in case you get lost or get stuck in traffic)

- Any important company information or product literature

- A copy of your CV

- Your diary (you may be asked about your availability for the next stage at the end of the interview)

- Pen and paper

- Your 'agenda' and any notes of any key points you want to make

- Any relevant references.

Being aware of body language

Yes, I know that you may have some awareness of body language already, but trust me, an interview is the place where all your personal body language 'tics' and unconscious signals will come out.

Firstly, there are many opinions and interpretations of the signals we give unconsciously, so it is important that you consider this aspect of communication. All of us do it all of the time, particularly in situations of stress or uncertain environments of which we are unfamiliar.

What follows is a generally accepted view on the subject but a word of caution is needed.

HOT TIP

Take care not to over-analyse and interpret non-verbal signals. Scratching your chin can sometimes just mean that you have an itch on your chin.

Secondly, and probably more importantly to those of you who hope to have an international travel aspect to your role, body language is culturally dependent. For example, we may interpret someone avoiding eye contact to be less than honest but, in a number of countries and cultures, it is expected behaviour when talking to someone you respect or of higher social status. Our bodies send out a continuous stream of signals and even silence can be loaded with unspoken meanings. We listen with our eyes as much as with our ears.

So, in your interview preparation, think about all of your communication.

'Body language' basics

Words

There have been numerous studies about how important words are in communication. Some suggest that the words people spoke contributed to less than **10% of the impact** or effectiveness in trying to force people's attitudes. Whether you agree with this, or not, it's important to remember this as a concept.

Voice

Loudness, softness, tone, tempo and inflection are generally accepted to account for somewhere between **35% and 40% of our impact**.

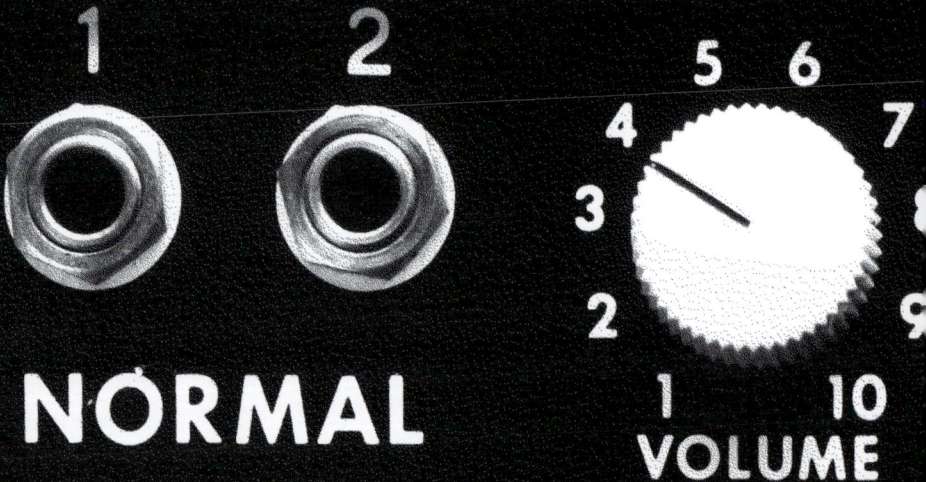

NORMAL

1 2 5 6 7 4 3 2 8 9 1 10
VOLUME

Body

Movement, posture, eye contact and facial expression, combined with overall appearance is suggested to contribute up to **55% of the impact** of our communication. To listen effectively you need to learn how to spot any underlying conflict, boredom or discomfort and should be aware of what we are saying with our posture and reduce any negative effects to a whisper rather than a shout.

Eyes

Our eyes are probably the best signal of how we are getting on with someone. Usually we look at people's eyes and faces to show we are listening or to get feedback on what we are saying.

If someone maintains eye contact whilst we are speaking, it is at least a signal that they are interested, even if they don't agree with what we are saying. In general conversation listeners look more at the speaker then vice versa.

Subconsciously, listeners are searching for cues that support or contradict the speaker's words. Are they lying? Are they serious? Should I laugh?

People also look at each other more in co-operative relationships and less if the relationship is tense or cold. People who are lying eventually avert their eyes and look down. Admittedly, some people can maintain their gaze when telling a lie but they usually overdo it and reveal a dishonesty with a long, fixed, unnatural stare.

Facial expression and body movements

Most facial expressions last for about half a second to a second. Some can't be caught by the most alert observer but most of us react to facial expressions intuitively, even if we can't explain what causes us to react that way.

When people like each other or are in agreement, their bodies tend to move at the same time or speed or in the same way. They tend to lean forward or backward at the same time, they use similar motions with the arms, legs and hands. People seated next to each other who are in agreement tend to cross and uncross their legs at about the same time and assume a similar sitting position.

When people don't agree, their body motion is reversed and the listener might slightly turn away from the speaker. Listeners in a positive mood tend to do things like scratching their chin, run fingers through their hair and look up at the ceiling. Feet and legs often reveal anxiety or even rage with tense posture and nervous leg jiggling.

Assuming a posture similar to someone standing or sitting nearby can reveal the desire to identify with them. In negotiations, people sit closer to the table if they are pleased with progress, or further from the table if the talks are either displeasing or frightening.

085

A QUICK WORD ABOUT telephone & skype

Much of our advice equally applies to telephone interviews. They key thing to remember is that, no matter how informal they say the conversation is, they'll be assessing you, so don't be seduced and say things you shouldn't.

Seize every chance you can to drive home your interest in the job and your relevant skills and experiences (it is even easier to use your pre-prepared agenda, as the interviewer can't see that you have one in front of you!). The other advice about how you present yourself still applies but with only your voice to sell you it is all the more important to be enthusiastic, relevant and all the other things you strive for in face-to-face meetings.

All of our advice is equally transferable to 'Skype' interviews, so you don't really need to do anything different, however, remember our three golden rules:

1. Do not be tempted to slouch – even in telephone interviews (the interviewer will be able to tell from your tone of voice).

2. On Skype, never, ever forget that you are being watched.

3. Remain professional and be fully prepared well before the call has started. Remain professional and in the 'interview zone' until you are absolutely sure that the interview has finished and the interviewer has logged off the call.

The behavioural or competency job interview

Behavioural, or competency job interviews, are increasingly common and, in my humble opinion, this is the area where genuine 'interview technique' applies. Standard interviews are not so much about technique, but actually about preparation and communication.

In a behavioural interview the interviewer asks specific questions seeking information about a candidate's skills, character and preferences based on examples of past behaviour. During the behavioural job interview, questions are directed toward specific experiences.

Our favourite description of an individual competence is a 'description of measurable work habits and personal skills used to achieve a work objective.' Some companies describe competencies as 'underlying characteristics, behaviours or skills required to differentiate performance' but, put simply, competencies are the key characteristics of the most successful performers that help them to be… well, successful.

Some examples:

" Tell me about a time when you had to work with a difficult person."

" What proactive steps have you taken to make your workplace more efficient and productive? Specifically describe a policy, project or system you created or initiated."

" Describe a high pressure situation you had to handle at work. Tell me what happened, who was involved and what you did in terms of problem solving."

" Some situations require us to express ideas or opinions in a very tactful and careful way. Tell me about a time when you were successful in this type of situation."

Most people can give an example to most behavioural questions that they are asked, but the trick is to give your 'best' example. This is where preparation comes in. At the end of this book we have included some typical behavioural interview questions collected in key themes. With a little bit of thought, and by looking at the job description and person specification, you should be able to identify the key themes or competencies that the interviewer will be trying to evidence. To make this easier, go through the job description line-by-line, and picture yourself doing the job. What will the person in the role be responsible for? What are the likely challenges?

Once you've done this you can set about spending some time thinking about your example. For each responsibility or challenge, think about what examples from your past you can point to as 'supporting evidence' that you'd excel at the job, and write them down.

The key here is to spend at least a couple of hours on this. Our experience tells us that your first example will never be your best, so take the time to come up with at least two or three examples for each 'theme' that you have predicted you will be asked about. This also helps if one of your examples applies to more than one theme, as it will help if you don't regurgitate the same example over and over again.

HOT TIP

Behavioural or competency interviews are where technique is as important as anything else.

How to answer a behavioural interview question

Firstly, don't respond to a behavioural interview question with an extended pause or by saying something like, "wow, that's a good question." By all means, repeat the question out loud or ask for the question to be repeated to give you a little more time to think about an answer. Also, a short pause before responding is okay.

Use all your life experiences as examples for your answers.

HOT TIP

When answering behavioural interview questions there are no right or wrong answers, so be honest. If you don't have an example for a question you're asked, don't try to make something up.

The S.T.A.R. method

Though this structure maybe familiar to you, I'll provide a quick recap here for the benefit of those who are unfamiliar. It's important that you understand this structure, as it will allow you to provide a detailed, articulate answer for even the most complex question. It will also assist you in ordering your thoughts, if and when you happen to be surprised by a question that you haven't prepared for in advance.

SITUATION
TASK
ACTIONS
RESULT

S.T.A.R. – a recap

Situation:	Describe in a sentence or two what the initial scenario was.
Task:	List as a set of verbal bullet points, the tasks you identified that needed to be achieved.
Actions:	Describe the actions you took to complete the tasks, in particular identifying any obstacles you overcame with a brief description of how.
Result:	Describe the end result. Don't worry about a less than perfect outcome in your example, as long as you can talk about what you learned from it and how you have used this experience since.

The structure itself is fairly self explanatory and provided you follow it step-by-step, it should allow you to deliver a clear answer for whatever question is presented to you.

Question ?

Describe a situation where you had a conflict with another individual, and how you dealt with it. What was the outcome?

Answer !

Situation or Task

During a previous role, I worked on a four person team that was ……. I got along with everyone quite well, except for one colleague. We disagreed strongly on the method we should use to …… My other teammates and I agreed on a course of action but he totally disagreed. He didn't budge on his position and even took passive-aggressive steps to prevent us from completing the project.

Action that you took

As a member of the team I set up an informal meeting. I simply asked him to explain his reasons for wanting to do the experiment his way. I just listened and asked questions to clarify. Some of his assumptions were clearly erroneous, but I knew pointing them out right away would just make him get defensive. After hearing him out, I had a better idea of where he was coming from and realised that he might have some misunderstandings on some basic concepts. I didn't think he would take too kindly to me correcting him, so I suggested that maybe we should set up a meeting with some other team members to discuss our different ideas and to see if he had any feedback or advice.

Result of the action

So we met with the other team members. We both presented our different reasons for wanting to do the experiment in a certain way. As predicted, the team brought up the faulty assumptions our stubborn teammate had, and that his method wouldn't be the best to use. He was obviously deflated, but he accepted the feedback and agreed to start using our method.

A QUICK WORD ABOUT
★ ★ ★
Psychometric testing
★ ★ ★

Put simply, psychometric tests are a scientific way of measuring performance. They are often seen as a much more objective way of assessing people and are frequently included as part of an interview process (most often ahead of final interview stage).

Personality profiling tools are commonly used during psychometric testing. These often include personality questionnaires and assessments of motivation and emotional intelligence. Your profile, as described by these assessments, can change over time and is affected by a number of factors including, rather obviously, your emotional state, your current role (and how much you enjoy it and are challenged by it), your current Line Manager (and your relationship with them) and a range of external non-work related factors.

As these tests are, by design, objective in nature, you should never try to cheat or manipulate your answers to what you think they are trying to evidence (most psychometric tests have an inbuilt ability to spot if you try and do this!). Instead, cast your mind to a recent day when you felt motivated, challenged and energised by your work, your colleagues and your team. This will help to paint a picture of your 'best' self.

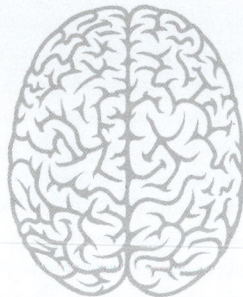

General interviews

It goes without saying that no two interviews are exactly the same and can be a mixture of styles, so it is important to be prepared. At the opposite extreme to a formal competency based interview, you may find yourself in an unstructured interview that can appear like a general chat. Whilst at first glance this can seem like an 'easy' interview, this actually is far from the case as you may leave the interviewer knowing everything about your football obsession or extreme shopping habits but nothing about your suitability for the job. In this case it is important to take SOME control and make sure prior to the interview you know the key elements you want to highlight regarding your experience and relevance for the role.

Other popular interview questions

No two situations are ever exactly the same, but as a general guide, certain types of questions come up in a typical interview time and time again. Here is our guide to some of those specific questions and our advice as to the things that they are trying to evidence and how you should tackle them.

1 Tell me about yourself

The question (if not directly) will almost certainly come up. Not preparing a succinct, well thought out, high quality answer to this question is <u>unforgivable</u> but very, very few individuals do!

The subject that you know most about in the whole world is yourself and so most of us presume that, as we are subject matter experts on us, we don't need to think about this… but wait a minute. This is half about content and half about perception. Irrelevant ramblings with no middle and no end to the story, or the answer, will give the interviewer a poor impression of you very early in the interview. You will be peddling up hill to recover for the next 50 minutes.

This question, often the interview opener, has a crucial objective: to see how you handle yourself in unstructured situations. The interviewer will want to see how articulate you are, how confident you are, and generally what type of impression you would make on the people with whom you come into contact on the job.

1 Tell me about yourself (continued)

Your response should never take more than two to three minutes. When asked to tell them about yourself, please do just tell them about yourself. DO NOT use this as an invitation to provide a monologue of everything they might want to know about why you are right for the job.

There are many ways to respond to this question correctly and just one wrong way: by asking, "What do you want to know?" The right response typically has three parts: focus on what interests the interviewer, highlight your most important accomplishments and prove that you are a human being.

Focus on what interests the interviewer

Do not dwell on your personal history - that is not why you are there. Start with your most recent employment and explain why you are well qualified for the position. The key to all successful interviews is to match your qualifications to what the interviewer is looking for. You want to be selling what the buyer is buying.

Highlight important accomplishments

Have a story ready that illustrates your best professional qualities. For example, if you tell an interviewer that people describe you as creative, provide a brief story that shows how you have been creative in achieving your goals.

Prove that you are a human being

This is the bit where you give a very brief overview of who you really are, giving the briefest of pictures of what matters to you out of work. This should be easy, however do give it some thought and a bit of craft to your answer.

Oh yes, and we do actually agree with you that attending Star Wars conventions dressed as Princess Leia at weekends is cool and that your collection of 1950s bottles tops is one of the best in the North of England, however please do understand that some people will find this just a bit weird, so it might not be the best place to start in an interview. We are not joking, this does happen when people say "tell me about yourself".

HOT TIP A good interviewee will memorise a 60-second commercial that clearly demonstrates why he, or she, is the best person for the job.

2 What do you do when you are not working?

With this question the interviewer is seeking a bit more information about who you are, the qualities that you can bring to their organisation and how you will fit with their existing team.

This links directly to the 'Prove you are a human being' part of the answer to question 1. The interviewer wants to try and judge whether you are happy and well-adjusted, or a company zealot.

Discuss hobbies or pursuits that interest you such as sports, clubs, cultural activities and favourite things to read, and don't mention Princess Leia and 1950s bottle tops!

3 What is your biggest weakness?

The key to responding to this question, perhaps rather obviously, is to avoid discussing characteristics critical to the position as a weakness. An impressive and confident response shows that the candidate has either prepared for the question, is seriously self-aware, has spent time on self-reflection, and can admit responsibility and accept constructive criticism.

Sincerely give an honest answer (but not a long one), be confident in the fact that this weakness does not make you any less of a great candidate, show that you are working on this weakness and tell the interviewer how. The best answers include how you have, or are, taking action to improve on your weaknesses and, in particular, what coping strategies you have employed to make sure that your employer or department isn't disadvantaged by this weakness.

4 What are your strengths?

The key to success is to demonstrate that you own strengths that are important to the specific job responsibilities. If the position requires scheduling or handling many deadlines, you should discuss your ability to multi-task, your use of collaboration or time management software, or give an example of a project you successfully managed.

Do not take this as an opportunity to open the flood gates and go through an exhaustive list of what makes the 'Super you'. Instead, describe two or three skills you have that are relevant to the job. Avoid clichés and generalities at all costs and make sure you offer specific evidence with examples answering the question of 'So what?'
If you really want to do a bit of showboating, describe new ways these skills could be put to use in the position you are being considered for.

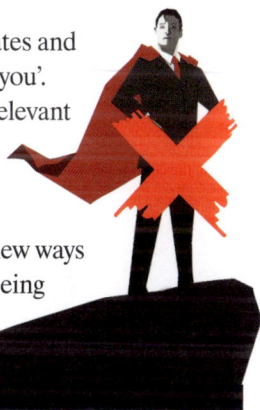

5 Why do you want to work for this company/in this industry?

Provide proof that you aren't simply shopping in this interview. Make your passion for your work a theme that you allude to continually throughout the interview.

If you already work in the sector and you are changing employers, do exactly the same but demonstrate that you have made an assessment of their organisation and have a clear, well thought out rationale for being interested in their organisation. Accuracy of your view is the key here. A misguided or misinformed view about a sector or business will kill your chances of success, so take time to think about why you really want to be there.

The end of the interview

Usually the interviewer will signal when the interview is coming to an end. Try and use this as an opportunity to take the initiative.

Checking through your pre-prepared agenda you had wanted to share your experience in advanced spreadsheet modelling, however, the topic was never brought up. It is your responsibility to introduce it into the conversation. You might comment, "Before we end, I'd like to share one more thing with you that I think is important to the position and my fit within your organisation." Then proceed with the information. You must take the initiative during an interview to be sure you have communicated all that is of value.

When the interview has finally ended, establish what will happen next and who should do what. Be sincere in your thanks, even if you've been given a rough ride. Reinforce your interest in the job, even if you have some reservations. The objective is to be offered the position as you can always turn a job down once it is offered!

"I'm very excited about this opportunity. What's our next step?"

This might very well be the deciding factor in getting an offer. And make sure that you actually SAY it in words at the end of the interview. Don't assume that they should have noticed your enthusiasm and interest level in this position from the rest of your comments during the interviewing process.

Establish what the next stage of the process is likely to be and what sort of timescales the interviewer is working towards. Now is also a good time to mention the subject of feedback. Something like:

"Thank you, I have really enjoyed this interview and have learnt a lot more about the position and organisation. I am obviously really keen however, should I not be successful, I would really value some feedback. If that is the case, what is the best way to do this?"

No, this isn't defeatist. The interviewer will probably have already made their mind up as to whether you will be coming back for another interview, so use this as an opportunity to try and line up some qualitative feedback. But, if you're asking for feedback, be prepared to deal with it. Egos are funny things and as well as not liking rejection, we tend to take details of that rejection pretty badly. Be pragmatic about this. Sometimes you did everything right and were just pipped to the post by someone working for a direct competitor that was just too good to turn down. Whether this is the case or not, anything you can glean as interview feedback will only serve to fine tune you for next time.

EXIT

In summary:

The three keys to effective interviewing are:

1: Preparation

2: Practice

3: Presentation

Preparation   ⓵

Prepare in advance of <u>every</u> interview

You simply cannot over-prepare for an interview. Those who prepare and take the time to do all their homework, put themselves at a major competitive advantage. Consider all the following steps in preparation for an up-coming interview:

Know the format

Confirm ahead of time the format of the interview. Will it be a phone interview, face-to-face interview, panel interview, lunch interview, etc? You NEVER want to be surprised by the format - it can definitely throw you off and affect your level of confidence.

Know the 'players'

Find out as much as you can about all of those individuals with whom you will be interviewing. Ask for their names in advance. If you're working with a recruiter, ask him or her to provide you with that information. Do a Google and LinkedIn search on all of the individuals. Look for things in common with your background – former employers, college and university alumni, professional organisations, outside interests, etc. Draw up a list of possible talking points.

Know the position

Make sure you thoroughly understand the roles and responsibilities of the position for which you will be interviewed. Ask for a job description, find out why the position is open, thoroughly research similar positions on the internet (job boards are a great resource for this exercise). Confirm your understanding of the position with your key contact at the company. Make no presumptions about the position.

In summary:

The three keys to
effective interviewing are:

1: Preparation

2: Practice

3: Presentation

101

Preparation (continued)   (1)

Research the company

Thoroughly research the company. Talk to those in your network who know the company. Research the company on the internet. If a public company, review publicly available financial statement information. What are the key issues currently facing the company? Why is the position you are interviewing for available? Is it a new position? If so, why? Is it a replacement position? If so, what happened to the former employee? What are the company's key strengths? What is their market share for key products/services? What is going on with the company's key competitors? What late-breaking news is available on the company? Set up a Google Alert for the weeks/days leading up to your interview to keep current on late-breaking news.

Draw up insightful questions

Make a list of GREAT questions that you can ask. Formulate separate sets of questions for each of the individuals that will be interviewing you. Orient your questioning to each person's background, role and responsibility at the company. Remember… Great questions = Great candidates.

Draw up a list of questions that will likely be asked of you

Put together a comprehensive list of some of the key questions that you are likely to be asked. What are the most difficult questions that you could be asked? Consider things such as: Gaps in your work experience; Short-tenure job positions (particularly those where you were employed less than one year); Lack of experience in one or more of the key requirements of the job position for which you will be interviewing.

In summary:

The three keys to effective interviewing are:

1: Preparation

2: Practice

3: Presentation

Practice (2)

This is the big one that most newly or recently qualified candidates fail to give sufficient attention to. My experience in working with hundreds and hundreds of candidates and preparing them for job interviews is that those who prepare almost always outshine their competition. Ideas for practice include:

- Role playing with a friend, your spouse, or an experienced coach.

- Self-observation. Practising in front of a mirror.

- Video replay. Video-taping yourself and critiquing your performance.

- Audio replay. Recording yourself and critiquing your performance.

As with anything, practice makes perfect. Why leave anything to chance? If the position you're planning to interview for is important, take the time to practise.

As an easy way into a practice session, why don't you get a friend, spouse/partner, or someone you know well, to randomly ask some of the interview questions at the back of this book?

In summary:

The three keys to effective interviewing are:

1: Preparation

2: Practice

3: Presentation

Presentation   3

Interview attire

Know the dress-style expectation ahead of time and take it up just a notch. If it's business casual and they ask you to dress business casual, then respect their request but take it up just a notch. For males that means putting a blue blazer over your golf shirt and wearing impeccable shoes.

Impeccable grooming speaks for itself.

Watch your manners

Show respect for everyone you meet; the Receptionist, the Administrative Assistant...everyone! It may be that everyone's vote counts. Be kind, be considerate, be nice.

Smile and be engaging

Interviews are serious, but let your personality come through. Smile and show enthusiasm. Be engaging. Practise an interview style that replaces 'stiffness' with being more conversational. Be interesting.

Avoid humour

Leave the joke-telling to others.

Appendix

Examples of Competency Based Interview questions

As an aid to your preparation we have attempted to cover some pretty typical competence areas and for each a number of example questions for you to practise. For the purpose of this appendix we have called these '**Competencies**' as they are very common. Have a go at answering some of the questions using the S.T.A.R. method.

Good Luck!

Competencies

Interview competency – Communication

Communicates effectively, listens sensitively, adapts communication to audience and fosters effective communication with others.

Verbal

- Tell us about a situation where your communication skills made a difference to a situation.

- Describe a time when you had to win someone over, who was reluctant or unresponsive.

- Describe a situation where you had to explain something complex to a colleague or a client. Which problems did you encounter and how did you deal with them?

- What is the worst communication situation that you have experienced?

- How do you prepare for an important meeting?

- Tell us about a situation when you failed to communicate appropriately.

- Demonstrate how you vary your communication approach according to the audience that you are addressing.

- Describe a situation when you had to communicate a message to someone, knowing that you were right and that they were wrong and reluctant to accept your point of view.

Competencies

Listening

- Give us an example where your listening skills proved crucial to an outcome.

- Tell us about a time when you were asked to summarise complex points.

- Tell us about a time when you had trouble remaining focused on your audience. How did you handle this?

- What place does empathy play in your work? Give an example where you needed to show empathy?

- Describe a situation where you had to deal with an angry customer.

Written

- What type of writing have you done? Give examples? What makes you think that you are good at it?

- How do you feel writing a report differs from preparing an oral presentation?

- What positive and negative feedback have you received about your writing skills? Give an example where one of your reports was criticised.

- How do you plan the writing of a report?

Competencies

Interview competency – Conflict management

Encourages creative tension and differences of opinions. Anticipates and takes steps to prevent counter-productive confrontations. Manages and resolves conflicts and disagreements in a constructive manner.

- Tell us about a time when you felt that conflict or differences were a positive driving force in your organisation. How did you handle the conflict to optimise its benefit?

- Tell us about a time when you had to deal with a conflict within your team.

- Tell us about a situation where conflict led to a negative outcome. How did you handle the situation and what did you learn from it?

- Give us an example where you were unable to deal with a difficult member of your team.

Interview competency – Decisiveness

Makes well-informed, effective, and timely decisions, even when data is limited or solutions produce unpleasant consequences; perceives the impact and implications of decisions.

- What big decision did you make recently? How did you go about it?

- How did you reach the decision that you wanted to change job?

- Give an example of a time when you had to delay a decision to reflect on the situation. Why did you need to do this?

Competencies

- What is the decision that you have put off the longest? Why?

- When was the last time that you refused to make a decision?

- Give us an example of a situation where you had to make a decision without the input of key players, but knowing that these key players would judge you on that decision (e.g. superior unavailable at the time).

- Tell us about a time when you had to make a decision without knowledge of the full facts.

- Tell us about a situation where you made a decision that involuntarily impacted negatively on others. How did you make that decision and how did you handle its consequences?

- Tell us about a decision that you made, which you knew would be unpopular with a group of people. How did you handle the decision-making process and how did you manage expectations?

- Tell us about a situation where you made a decision too quickly and got it wrong. What made you take that decision?

Competencies

Interview competency – Delegation

Able to make full and best use of subordinate, providing appropriate support.

- What type of responsibilities do you delegate? Give examples of projects where you made best use of delegation.

- Give an example of a project or task that you felt compelled to complete on your own. What stopped you from delegating?

- Give an example of a situation where you reluctantly delegated to a colleague. How did you feel about it?

- Give an example where you delegated a task to the wrong person. How did you make that decision at the time, what happened and what did you learn from it?

- How do you cope with having to go away from the office for long periods of time (e.g. holidays)? Explain how you would delegate responsibilities based on your current situation.

Competencies

Interview competency – Influencing

Ability to convince others to own expressed point of view, gain agreement and acceptance of plans, activities or products.

- Describe a situation where you were able to influence others on an important issue. What approaches or strategies did you use?

- Describe a situation where you needed to influence different stakeholders who had different agendas. What approaches or strategies did you use?

- Tell us about an idea that you managed to sell to your superior, which represented a challenge.

- What is your worst selling experience?

- Describe the project or idea that you were most satisfied to sell to your management.

- Describe a time where you failed to sell an idea that you knew was the right one.

Competencies

Interview competency – Integrity

Ability to maintain job related, social, organisational and ethical norms.

- When have you had to lie to achieve your aims? Why did you do so? How do you feel you could have achieved the same aim in a different way?

- Tell me about a time when you showed integrity and professionalism.

- Tell us about a time when someone asked you something that you objected to. How did you handle the situation?

- Have you ever been asked to do something illegal, immoral or against your principles? What did you do?

- What would you do if your boss asked you to do something illegal?

- Tell me about a situation where you had to remind a colleague of the meaning of 'integrity'.

Competencies

Interview competency – Leadership

Acts as a role model. Anticipates and plans for change. Communicates a vision to a team.

- Tell us about a situation where you had to get a team to improve its performance. What were the problems and how did you address them?

- Describe a time when you had to drive a team through change. How did you achieve this?

- Describe a situation where you needed to inspire a team. What challenges did you meet and how did you achieve your objectives?

- Tell us about a situation where you faced reluctance from your team to accept the direction that you were setting.

- Describe a project or situation where you had to use different leadership styles to reach your goal.

- Tell me about a time when you were less successful as a leader than you would have wanted to be.

Competencies

Interview competency – Resilience and tenacity

Deals effectively with pressure; remains optimistic and persistent, even under adversity. Recovers quickly from setbacks. Stays with a problem/line of thinking until a solution is reached or is no longer reasonably attainable.

- Tell us about a situation where things deteriorated quickly. How did you react to recover from that situation?

- Tell us about a project where you achieved success despite the odds being stacked against you. How did you ensure that you pulled through?

- Tell us about your biggest failure. How did you recover and what have you learnt from that incident?

- Give us an example of a situation where you knew that a project or task would place you under great pressure. How did you plan your approach and remain motivated?

- How do you deal with stress?

- Give us an example of a situation where you worked under pressure.

- Under what conditions do you work best and worst?

- Which recent project or situation has caused you the most stress? How did you deal with it?

- Why did you last lose your temper?

- When is the last time that you were upset with yourself?

- What makes you frustrated or impatient at work?

- What is the biggest challenge that you have faced in your career? How did you overcome it?

Competencies

- Tell us about a time when you wanted to push one of your ideas successfully, despite strong opposition.

- Which course or topics have you found most difficult? How did you address the challenge?

Interview competency – Teamwork

Contributes fully to the team effort and plays an integral part in the smooth running of a team without necessarily taking the lead.

- Describe a situation in which you were a member of a team. What did you do to positively contribute to it?

- Tell us about a situation where you played an important role in a project as a member of the team (not as a leader).

- How did you ensure that every member of the team was allowed to participate?

- Give us an example where you worked in a dysfunctional team. Why was it dysfunctional and how did you attempt to change things?

- Give an example of a time when you had to deal with a conflict within your team. What did you do to help resolve the situation?

- How do you build relationships with other members of your team?

- How do you bring difficult colleagues on board? Give us an example where you had to do this.